D1715940

HISTORY OF CRIME AND PUNISHMENT

FOR-PROFIT PRISONS

BY DUCHESS HARRIS, JD, PHD
WITH CYNTHIA KENNEDY HENZEL

Essential Library

An Imprint of Abdo Publishing | abdobooks.com

ABDOBOOKS.COM

Published by Abdo Publishing, a division of ABDO, PO Box 398166, Minneapolis, Minnesota 55439. Copyright © 2020 by Abdo Consulting Group, Inc. International copyrights reserved in all countries. No part of this book may be reproduced in any form without written permission from the publisher. Essential Library™ is a trademark and logo of Abdo Publishing.

Printed in the United States of America, North Mankato, Minnesota.
022019
092019

Interior Photos: Matt Rourke/AP Images, 5, 8; Kristen Mullen/The Citizen's Voice/ AP Images, 10; North Wind Picture Archives, 15; AP Images, 17; Charles Tasnadi/ AP Images, 20; Andrew Lichtenstein/Corbis News/Getty Images, 27, 38, 55; Rich Pedroncelli/AP Images, 29, 67; Jim Cole/AP Images, 35; Dennis M. Rivera Pichardo/ Bloomberg/Getty Images, 41; J. Scott Applewhite/AP Images, 45; J. David Ake/ AP Images, 49; Mark Rogers/Lubbock Avalanche-Journal/AP Images, 52–53; Bebeto Matthews/AP Images, 57; Melanie Stetson Freeman/The Christian Science Monitor/Getty Images, 62; Jim Grant/Nevada Appeal/AP Images, 65; Corey Lowenstein/The News & Observer/AP Images, 71; Red Line Editorial, 73; Jacquelyn Martin/AP Images, 76; Eric Risberg/AP Images, 79; Eric Gay/AP Images, 81, 87; Sue Ogrocki/AP Images, 91; Franck Crusiaux/Gamma-Rapho/Getty Images, 96

Editor: Charly Haley
Series Designer: Dan Peluso

LIBRARY OF CONGRESS CONTROL NUMBER: 2018965870

PUBLISHER'S CATALOGING-IN-PUBLICATION DATA

Names: Harris, Duchess, author | Henzel, Cynthia Kennedy, author.
Title: For-profit prisons / by Duchess Harris and Cynthia Kennedy Henzel
Description: Minneapolis, Minnesota : Abdo Publishing, 2020 | Series: History of
    crime and punishment | Includes online resources and index.
Identifiers: ISBN 9781532119187 (lib. bdg.) | ISBN 9781532173363 (ebook)
Subjects: LCSH: Prisons--United States--Juvenile literature. | Prisons--Finance--Law
    and legislation--Juvenile literature. | Privatization--Law and legislation--
    Juvenile literature. | Corrections--Contracting out--United States--Juvenile
    literature. | Administration of criminal justice--Juvenile literature.
Classification: DDC 364.6097--dc23

CONTENTS

CHAPTER ONE

KIDS FOR CASH

Hillary Transue speaks to a news reporter in her Pennsylvania home about her experience being sent to a for-profit juvenile prison as part of the Kids for Cash scandal.

n April 2007, 15-year-old Hillary Transue and some of her

friends thought it would be funny to create a social media

page making fun of their high school's assistant principal.

Transue, an honor student, created the page. But school

officials didn't think it was funny, and they called the police.

Transue was criminally charged with harassment in Luzerne

County, Pennsylvania. A court date was set.

Transue's mother was a former social worker, so she

understood the criminal justice system—or at least she

thought she did. She expected that her daughter would be

reprimanded and at most sentenced to community service.

After all, Transue had never been in trouble before. When

Transue and her mother arrived at court, they were asked

whether they had a lawyer. They said they did not, and they

YOUTH INCARCERATION

Of the almost 2.3 million people in the United States held in confinement, approximately 53,000 are younger than 18. Most of these youths are held in juvenile facilities, but 5,000 are in adult facilities. Approximately 2,300 youths are held for status offenses, which are crimes that apply only to juveniles, such as truancy or underage drinking. Other young people, approximately 8,600, are in jail for violating their parole. Approximately 6,000 youths are incarcerated for public order offenses, which are actions that disrupt public order, such as carrying a weapon in public. Other crimes for which youths are incarcerated include drug offenses (2,600), property crimes such as arson or theft (10,400), and person offenses, which are crimes against another person, such as assault, robbery, or homicide (18,100).[1] As of 2015, approximately half of the juvenile detention facilities in the United States were run by state or local governments. The other half were private facilities. Some of those private detention facilities were run by nonprofit organizations, such as churches or youth rehabilitation organizations. Others were run by for-profit businesses to make money.

assumed that a public defender, which is a court-appointed lawyer, would be provided to represent Transue. They were given a document to sign. Transue's mom thought it was the paperwork required for a public defender, so she signed it.

At the courthouse, several young people and their parents waited to appear before the judge. When it was Transue's turn, she and her mother were met with a surprise—there was no lawyer waiting for them. They later discovered that the paper Transue's mother signed had actually said they did not want a lawyer.

Transue finally stood before Luzerne County judge Mark Ciavarella to answer questions. Ciavarella had been elected because he was considered tough on crime. He believed kids should be treated harshly to prevent them from committing further offenses. After less than a minute of questioning, Ciavarella sentenced Transue to be incarcerated for three months. A guard led Transue away in handcuffs to join the hundreds of other young people in PA Child Care, a new private prison for juvenile offenders.

A FOUNDATION FOR CORRUPTION

Transue and her mother were in shock. Transue had played a prank and then apologized for her poor judgment. But now she was in prison and would have a record as a juvenile delinquent. Transue's mother contacted a lawyer, but Ciavarella refused to hear an appeal. She called the American Civil Liberties Union (ACLU), but the national advocacy organization didn't want to get involved in the case.

Finally, Transue's mother called the Juvenile Law Center of Pennsylvania. The nonprofit law firm had already raised concerns about Ciavarella in the past. It filed a motion to the state supreme court on behalf of about 500 juveniles who had appeared in court before Ciavarella without representation from a lawyer.[2] Under US law, all people have the right to legal representation when charged with a crime.

Later that year, as federal agents began investigating the treatment of juveniles in Judge Ciavarella's court, they

PA Child Care was the for-profit juvenile detention center associated with the Kids for Cash scandal.

discovered much more than a tough judge. They found a scheme between two judges and the local for-profit prison to make money by sentencing juveniles to jail. The scandal became known as Kids for Cash.

This is how Kids for Cash worked: In 2002, Luzerne County president judge Michael Conahan shut down an old juvenile detention center due to its poor conditions. He claimed the only alternative was to build a for-profit prison for young people. A for-profit prison is a private business that contracts with the local, state, or federal government to house inmates. Inmates may include people convicted of crimes, suspects awaiting trial who cannot afford to get out of jail on bond, or undocumented immigrants awaiting decisions on their status in the country. Some for-profit prisons are built to incarcerate juveniles. Separate for-profit facilities are built for adults.

Conahan put together an investment group to build a juvenile detention facility called PA Child Care. He contracted with a local developer to build the facility and with another contractor to run the facility. Contractors that operate for-profit prisons get paid for each person housed in their prison. More prisoners mean more profit for these companies.

To that end, keeping the prison full was Judge Ciavarella's job. He began sentencing juveniles to prison for minor crimes. He also started giving longer sentences to other juveniles. For their part in the scheme, the two judges were paid $2.6 million.

THE CHARGES

Once the scheme was discovered, the federal government charged Ciavarella and Conahan with numerous crimes including racketeering and money laundering. Conahan decided to plead guilty rather than face a jury trial. He was

Former Luzerne County Judge Mark Ciavarella speaks to reporters outside the courthouse after his trial.

sentenced to 17 years in prison. Ciavarella refused to admit he had done anything wrong. He went to trial.

In 2011, a jury convicted Ciavarella of 12 crimes. The judge sentenced him to 28 years in prison, and he had to pay $1 million in restitution. The lawyer who owned the prison facilities, Robert Powell, served 18 months in prison for paying bribes to judges. He later paid $4.75 million in a civil case. The other businessman involved in the scheme, property developer Robert Mericle, paid more than $17 million and served one year in prison. Of the thousands of kids Judge Ciavarella sentenced, 2,480 of the convictions were reversed or removed from the court records.[3]

Hillary Transue was released after spending three weeks in prison. She felt like everyone believed she was a juvenile delinquent—and, for a while, she believed it too. Yet Transue eventually graduated from high school and went on to college. Others were not so lucky. Some,

CHILDREN IN THE SYSTEM

Approximately two million children are arrested each year in the United States. That is five times more than in any other country. The vast majority of the arrests, 95 percent, are for nonviolent crimes ranging from shoplifting to drug possession.[4] When children are arrested, they often suffer many consequences beyond incarceration. Children may be ostracized in their community after they are released from jail. Sixty-six percent of the kids who are incarcerated never return to school.[5] In addition, families may face high legal fees that they can't afford.

traumatized by the experience, did not return to school. Seventeen-year-old Edward Kenzakoski, sentenced by Judge Ciavarella to nine months for possession of drug paraphernalia, came out of prison angry and traumatized. In an interview with CNN, his mother, Sandy Fonzo, said, "He was never the same. He went in a young boy, a young, spirited boy, and came out a pent-up, angry man."[6] Kenzakoski killed himself when he was 23. His mother blames Ciavarella for her son's death.

FOR-PROFIT PRISONS

Prisons play a significant role in American life. The United States has more people in prison than any other country in the world. As of 2018, there were approximately 2.3 million people in US prisons, while the country's total population was approximately 328 million.[7] Although the United States has less than 5 percent of the world's population, it has 25 percent of the world's prisoners.[8]

"A PICTURE OF SUCH HORROR"

Walnut Grove Correctional Facility, a juvenile prison in Mississippi known for its violence and poor living conditions, was run by a series of for-profit companies. Juveniles were removed from the facility in 2012 after a lawsuit in which the judge declared that the facility was "a picture of such horror as should be unrealized anywhere in the civilized world."[9] Adults were still kept at the prison until 2015, when the facility was closed entirely.

There are varying opinions on the role prisons should play in society. Some people believe prisons exist for public protection. They think violent criminals would commit more crimes if they were not locked up. Other people believe prisons should be a place to rehabilitate criminals. In this sense, prisons should offer job training, education, and therapy that will help inmates lead productive lives once their prison sentences are finished. Still others believe that crime deserves punishment and that prisons provide the means for that punishment.

However, for-profit prisons have a reason to exist beyond rehabilitating or punishing criminals. For-profit prisons make more money when they have more inmates. This monetary incentive has been known to cause corruption.

DISCUSSION STARTERS

- Do you believe that sending people to prison is a deterrent to crime? Why or why not?
- How do you think going to prison might change a young person?
- Who do you believe should operate prisons?

CHAPTER TWO

PRISONERS FOR PROFIT

An inmate at a New York jail in the 1890s

Housing people convicted of crimes and sentenced to prison is the responsibility of the government. Some prisons are run directly by the government. Other prisons are run by companies that contract with the government. Contracting private companies or individuals to run prisons is not new in the United States. The practice can be traced back to leasing convicts for labor in the 1800s. As early as 1825, Kentucky's state government leased the Kentucky State Penitentiary to a businessman, Joel Scott. In return for housing, feeding, and, if needed, disciplining the inmates to force them to work, Scott agreed to give the state half of the profits he made from the inmates' labor. In 1851, the state of California leased San Quentin Prison to two businessmen. After rampant corruption and mismanagement, as well as a change in the private management, California tried to break its contract with the businessmen running the prison. The businessmen went to court. The state was finally forced to pay $275,000 to return the prison to state control in 1860.

The Thirteenth Amendment to the US Constitution, passed in 1865 to abolish slavery, states that "involuntary servitude [is illegal], except as a punishment for crime whereof the party shall have been duly convicted."[1] After the

Civil War (1861–1865), farmers and business owners in the South did not know who would fill the jobs they had once forced upon unpaid slaves. They found a source for cheap labor in state prisons.

In 1868, the state of Georgia leased prisoners to railroad builders. The railroads paid $2,500 for 100 convicts to build the rails.[2] In 1869, Louisiana leased convict labor from Louisiana State Penitentiary to businessman Samuel James. He housed prisoners at a former plantation called Angola. These prisoners worked on Mississippi River levees. By 1885, 13 states contracted their prisoners to private companies.[3] Leased convicts worked in some of the country's most dangerous jobs, including mining and logging. In the 1870s, 45 percent of convicts in South Carolina who were leased to railroads died.[4]

Railroad builders were among the first for-profit companies to use prison labor.

Most prisoners at this time were black people who had previously been enslaved. Many people argue that in this sense, leased convict labor was an extension of slavery. After slavery was made illegal, people who stayed at home on their previous owners' properties were arrested on charges of trespassing or loitering. Additionally, harsh prison sentences for minor crimes mainly targeted former slaves. As a result, many former slaves simply returned to their work on plantations as convicts. They often experienced dangerous working conditions and received low wages.

PRISON LABOR TODAY

Prison inmates continue to work for low wages today. They may be employed within prisons or work for local governments doing tasks such as repairing streets or mowing grass. The median wage for state inmates is 20 cents per hour. Federal inmates average 31 cents per hour. Prisons do not fall under the Fair Labor Standards Act, a federal law that sets the minimum wage for employees. As of 2018, the federal minimum wage was $7.25 per hour. Some prisoners may work at regular jobs under work-release programs. These programs allow inmates to leave prison for their jobs and then return to confinement when they are not at work.

NEW LAWS

Prisoners contracted to private businesses were often mistreated and kept in inhumane conditions. Poor food, extreme punishments such as whippings, and crowded conditions were common. Due to newspaper accounts of these conditions and the public outcry that resulted, lawmakers began to respond to the problems.

Congress passed a law on February 23, 1887, forbidding federal prisons to lease prisoners to private companies. In the next few years, many states passed laws against state prisons leasing prisoners. Although this meant that private businesses could not profit directly from the labor of inmates, it did not mean that prisoners were not forced to work. Government-run prisons still used cheap inmate labor to produce goods, from canned food to furniture, to help pay for the cost of running prisons. Private businesses could not compete with the prices of goods made with cheap labor in prisons. The labor costs of businesses made their goods too expensive. Some states passed laws regulating the sale of goods produced in prisons so they would not hinder private businesses. Others did not.

In the late 1920s, Congress acted to protect businesses from the threat of cheap prison labor. In 1929, the Hawes-Cooper Act made goods produced in out-of-state prisons subject to the laws of the state in which they were sold. Going a step further, the Ashurst-Sumners Act in 1935 made it a federal offense to sell goods made in prisons in states where prison-made goods were prohibited. In 1940, Congress amended the Ashurst-Sumners Act to prohibit transporting goods made in prisons for private use. Prisons continued making goods that the government was already producing, such as car license plates. But cheap prison labor did not compete with business. It seemed that the days of private prisons or using prisoners for profit were in the past.

GETTING TOUGH ON CRIME

In the 1960s, Vietnam War (1955–1975) protests, the black power movement, and the civil rights movement all resulted in violent clashes in the United States between police and citizens. With riots in the streets and drug use rising, many people were concerned about public safety. Still, the number of people in prisons declined. The California prison population dropped by 25 percent from 1963 to 1972. In the first years of the 1970s, New York had its smallest prison population since 1950. The federal government prepared to close several prisons that were no longer needed. Congress

In the 1960s and 1970s, crowds of people gathered to protest the Vietnam War. The demonstrations sometimes resulted in violence.

voted in 1970 to eliminate most mandatory minimum sentences that required minimum prison terms for drug crimes. Most people thought drug addiction was a public health problem, not a criminal justice one. Eliminating the mandatory minimums allowed judges more discretion, such as the choice to give a lower sentence to a first-time offender.

Still, crime was a problem, especially drug-related crime, and many people wanted the government to do something about it. Nelson Rockefeller, the governor of New York from 1959 to 1973, had been progressive in his policies. He had favored drug rehabilitation instead of prison time. However, Rockefeller wanted the Republican Party nomination for president, and his policies were too liberal for many Republicans. So, he changed his ideas. In 1973, he advocated for what are known as the Rockefeller Laws—harsh sentences for crimes, especially crimes related to drugs. This stance became known as "tough on crime."

Part of Rockefeller's tough-on-crime policies encouraged mandatory minimum sentences. The New York legislature passed new laws that included a minimum sentence of 15 years in prison for selling more than two ounces (57 g) of drugs. This could be any type of drug, from heroin to marijuana. People possessing four ounces (113 g) or more of drugs all got the same mandatory sentence. Rockefeller became vice president of the United States in 1974.

In the 1970s, Governor Ronald Reagan of California also encouraged these tough-on-crime laws in his state. When he was elected president of the United States in 1980, he bolstered the federal War on Drugs. Congress passed the Comprehensive Crime Control Act of 1984, which increased penalties for drug crimes. It instituted new federal mandatory minimum sentences and three-strikes-and-you're-out laws. Under these laws, any person convicted of a third crime, no matter how small, would be sent to prison as opposed to being put on probation or simply being fined. The new laws also discouraged inmate release on parole.

CHANGING POLICIES

New crime laws can make a huge difference in prison populations. For-profit prisons have lobbied for laws that increase the number of prisoners and the length of prison sentences. Laws such as mandatory minimums, or mandated sentences for certain crimes, mean that judges essentially cannot choose the sentence for someone convicted of those crimes, even if a judge believes the sentence is too harsh. In 2003, Attorney General John Ashcroft pushed for federal prosecutors to charge people with crimes that had mandatory minimum sentences whenever possible. The federal prison population grew by about 48,000 people over the next ten years.[5] In 2013, Attorney General Eric Holder reversed the policy, encouraging prosecutors to file charges in a way that put only the worst criminals under mandatory sentencing guidelines. Nonviolent drug offenders without gang affiliations or a history of selling drugs to minors could get lighter sentences. The federal prison population fell for the first time in 40 years.[6] Jeff Sessions, who became attorney general in 2017, pushed for prosecutors to return to charging people with crimes that have the toughest penalties possible.

THE SOARING PRISON POPULATION

With these new laws, states and the federal government began incarcerating more people for longer periods of time. The prison and jail population across the United States soared. Prisons, generally run by states or the federal government, are facilities that house people convicted of crimes. Jails, usually run by cities or counties, house people who are awaiting trial or who are serving short sentences. In 1970, there were approximately 338,000 people incarcerated in prisons and jails. That number had increased by 136,000 by 1980. By 1990, there were more than one million people incarcerated in the United States.[7]

Governments had to find a way to house these new prisoners. But voters did not want to spend tax money on prisons. In the 1980s, voters rejected 60 percent of state and local attempts to use public funds to build new prisons.[8] Voters wanted politicians to be tough on crime, but they were not willing to pay for the results.

When Mario Cuomo was elected governor of New York in 1982, he faced a difficult situation. The number of people incarcerated in New York had doubled in less than a decade.[9] The state's prisons were dangerously overcrowded.

Voters would not approve new public funding for prisons. So Cuomo built more prisons by diverting funds from other projects. The same thing happened in other states and in the federal prison system as prison sentences became longer.

OVERCROWDING

As existing prisons became seriously overcrowded, inmates began to file lawsuits because of their deteriorating living conditions. In a 1982 case, the Tennessee prison system was ordered to reduce its prison population to the number of inmates that its prisons were designed to hold. The court also mandated that the state must provide adequate medical care, sanitary living conditions, and job training for prisoners. But Tennessee did not have money to build new prisons.

By the next year, the ACLU reported that eight states had prison systems that had been found to violate the Eighth Amendment to the US Constitution, which outlaws "cruel and unusual punishment." Seven additional states were waiting for court decisions about their prisons. Additionally, 21 states had individual prisons or jails that violated the Eighth Amendment.[10]

In 2001, the Prison Law Office, a nonprofit law firm in California, filed a lawsuit on behalf of Marciano Plata and several other prisoners. The lawsuit claimed that the overcrowded conditions in prisons were unconstitutional. In the case *Brown v. Plata*, the Supreme Court ruled in favor of the prisoners. The ruling said California had to reduce its prison population from 200 percent of capacity down to 137.5 percent of capacity. This meant the state had to build new prisons or release between 38,000 and 46,000 prisoners. As prisons' overcrowding and poor living conditions continued to be exposed in court, state prison systems had to do something.

BROWN V. PLATA

The Supreme Court was split in the case of *Brown v. Plata*, which ordered the state of California to reduce its prison population from 200 percent of capacity to 137.5 percent of capacity. Five justices agreed that overcrowding in prisons resulted in cruel and unusual punishment, which is banned by the US Constitution. However, four justices disagreed, stating that the Constitution does not give federal judges the right to oversee conditions in state prisons.

DISCUSSION STARTERS

- Do you think drug abuse is a public health issue, a criminal problem, or both?
- Why do you think voters wanted more people locked up but were opposed to paying to build more prisons?
- Do you think putting more people in prison makes the country safer? Why or why not?

CHAPTER THREE

THE RETURN OF PRIVATE PRISONS

All prisons have many methods of security, such as high fences or walls.

P rivate prisons got a bad reputation in the late 1800s, largely because of the mistreatment of prisoners. Many people considered private prisons a continuation of slavery after the Civil War. So, the country slowly went back to government-run facilities. But companies still made money on prisons. Public prisons commonly contracted with private businesses to provide services such as transporting prisoners, food preparation, medical care, and job training for inmates.

In the 1980s, three entrepreneurs, Thomas Beasley, Robert Crants, and T. Don Hutto, saw the growing prison population as an economic opportunity. In 1983, they formed the Corrections Corporation of America (CCA) to run for-profit prisons. Their new business venture would change the prison system for decades to come. In 1984, CCA signed its first contract. It would run the Silverdale Detention Center in Tennessee. The company soon opened another facility in Texas.

Then in 1985, as Tennessee was desperate to follow the 1982 court order to reduce overcrowding in its prisons, CCA proposed taking over the entire prison system in Tennessee for the next 99 years. The bold proposal raised concerns. What was the responsibility of the state regarding prisons, and what could be turned over to a private business? Who

The employment of guards and correctional officers is one of the many responsibilities that are transferred to a for-profit company when a public prison becomes private.

was responsible if someone escaped? Were prisons a public service like garbage collection, which was commonly contracted to private companies?

Opponents of the plan voiced concerns about the responsibility of the state to protect a prisoner's civil rights. This responsibility, they said, could not be handed off to a private company. They were also concerned about giving private employees, the correctional officers hired by CCA, the power to provide input into whether prisoners received parole. Plus, there was no guarantee that CCA would continue in the private prison business if it could not make a profit. The state might be left with thousands of prisoners and no personnel with the expertise to manage them. Tennessee decided not to turn over its entire prison system to CCA. However, the state contracted with the company to build and run two new prisons in the state.

That same year, CCA remodeled a hotel in Houston, Texas, to hold immigrant detainees for the federal government. Immigrant detainees are people who have not been convicted of any crime but who are formally suspected by the government of being in the country illegally. They are detained as they await court decisions about their immigration statuses.

THE GROWTH OF AN INDUSTRY

Another company, Wackenhut Corrections Corporation (later known as GEO Group), formed in 1984. It received its first contract in 1987 to house immigrant detainees for the federal government. The idea of private prisons caught on. By 1990, 7,000 prisoners were housed in for-profit prisons.[1]

Meanwhile, the flow of people into prisons accelerated. In 1994, President Bill Clinton signed the Violent Crime Control and Law Enforcement Act. This law provided billions of dollars in grants to states and cities for hiring

CHANGING NAMES

Ninety-six percent of the for-profit prison business in the United States is controlled by three companies—CoreCivic, GEO Group, and Management and Training Corporation (MTC).[2] All of these companies were founded in the 1980s, but some have changed their names since then. Corrections Corporation of America (CCA) became CoreCivic in 2016. In 2017, CoreCivic made $1.77 billion in revenue with profits of $516 million.[3] Damon Hininger, the chief executive officer (CEO), was paid $3.4 million in 2015. That is 19 times more than the salary of the director of the Federal Bureau of Prisons.[4] Wackenhut Corrections Corporation, formed in 1984, became the GEO Group in 2003. Since then, the company has acquired many other companies to expand its facilities and move into other services such as prison transport, inmate medical and mental health care, prison education, and post-prison services such as electronic monitoring. In 2017, GEO had revenues of $2.3 billion with profits of $563 million.[5] Its CEO, George Zoley, made almost $5 million in 2016.[6] The third large corporation, MTC, was founded in 1981.

new police officers and strengthening crime prevention programs. The money was also used to increase the country's border security.

This new law also enforced tough-on-crime laws. It increased penalties for drug offenses and violent crimes. It mandated three-strikes laws for drug trafficking or violent offenses. Mandatory minimums for sex crimes were doubled, and juveniles older than 13 could now be tried as adults for certain offenses.

The 1994 law was a boon for the for-profit prison industry. It provided the potential for huge numbers of new inmates and longer prison sentences. It also provided billions of dollars to fund prisons, including to build new facilities. Some of these new facilities were run by the government, while others were for-profit prisons. Half of the money for new facilities was set aside for states that enacted what were known as truth-in-sentencing laws, which required people convicted of violent crimes to serve at least 85 percent of their sentences before they could become eligible for parole.

States and the federal government began working with private companies to build new prisons. Most of the private prisons were built in rural areas in southern and western states. By 2010, for-profit prisons held 126,000 inmates, making up 9 percent of all state and federal prisoners.[7]

HOW FOR-PROFIT PRISONS WORK

Taxpayers pay for housing and caring for prisoners whether the inmates are in government-run prisons or for-profit prisons. A 2012 study by the Vera Institute of Justice found that the average cost of incarceration is $31,286 per prisoner per year.[8] Government prisons use tax dollars directly to pay for correctional officers and other prison personnel, food and medicine, education, and facility maintenance. Governments may contract out certain services, such as inmate job training, to private companies. But the business of running the prison is the responsibility of the government, and public prison employees are government workers.

Private prisons contract with federal, state, or local governments to house and care for prisoners. They may take over existing prisons that are owned by the government. They may use other buildings such as old hotels or even shopping malls to hold detainees if space is not available in existing facilities. In other cases, private companies may build new facilities. In lease-to-own deals, the new facilities are leased to the government until the cost of the facility, plus interest, is paid by the government. The facility then becomes publicly owned.

For-profit prisons contract with governments for operating a prison at a set price. The price for this service is determined as a certain number of dollars per inmate per day, an amount known as a bed rate. It is the responsibility of the company to hire guards and other prison personnel, plus provide food, clothing, and services such as medical care and job training to the inmates.

YOUTH IN DETENTION

Youth Services International (YSI) is a private company that operates juvenile detention centers. Investigations at its facilities in Florida have shown that they do not always provide enough food or basic supplies such as toilet paper. At some of the facilities, staff members had coaxed inmates to fight and failed to report claims of assaults and sexual abuse. At one facility, Thompson Academy, 96 percent of the staff had quit within a year. Youth counselors at the facility who work with inmates earned about $10.50 an hour in 2010.[9] In 2016, after almost two decades of reports of mistreatment of kids in its facilities, YSI lost its contracts to run juvenile detention facilities in Florida.[10]

The price that companies charge per bed varies depending on where the prison is located and other costs. CCA's first contract with Silverdale Detention Center charged the government $21 per day for each inmate. That was $3 less than what it cost the county to house an inmate at that time.[11] In 2014, CoreCivic (formerly CCA) charged Winn Correctional Center in Louisiana $34 per inmate per day. At that time, the estimated cost of housing an inmate in the public state prison was $52 per day. Some states pay private prisons as much as $80 per day to house a prisoner.[12]

For-profit prisons are supposed to provide the same services as public prisons. So, if the goal is to save money, it may seem like a good deal for governments to pay for-profit corporations to run prisons. It costs the taxpayers less. But, in addition to guarding and caring for prisoners, for-profit corporations must make money for their investors. How can they do this if they are charging rates cheaper than what it costs governments to run their own prisons?

WHERE THE PROFITS COME FROM

One reason for-profit prisons say they have an advantage is that private companies can make decisions, change policies, and innovate faster than governments. Government decisions often require going through several channels of approval or allowing for public input, all of which can slow down the process.

The most expensive part of running a prison is labor costs. Labor accounts for 65 to 70 percent of all expenses.[13] Private prisons do not have to hire union labor as government-run facilities do. Therefore, private prisons pay employees less. The average correctional officer at a government-run prison in the United States makes $36 per hour plus overtime, pensions, paid vacation days or sick

One of the highest expenses for prisons is the cost of paying guards and other staff members.

days, and health-care benefits. Private prisons, on average, pay correctional officers $14 per hour, and the workers may not receive many benefits or get paid for overtime.[14] At one facility, CoreCivic had too few correctional officers, security supervisors, and noncustody staff—fewer than what was required by its contract—so the company was fined $24,000. The fines were also a consequence of the facility keeping inmates beyond their release dates so it could charge for extra days. However, for the company, paying the fines was cheaper than reconciling these problems.

Most of the contracts that for-profit prisons sign with governments require that the facilities run by the corporations have a minimum occupancy. In these contracts, for-profit corporations require governments to pay penalties if prison beds are empty. This protects the company from fluctuations in the prison population, and therefore fluctuations in profits, due to changing laws or policies. Of course, governments want to avoid paying the penalty for not meeting minimum numbers of prisoners. In Tennessee, taxpayers paid $487,000 for empty beds at a female prison between 2011 and 2013 because the occupancy rate at a for-profit prison was at 90 percent, less than the contracted rate.[15]

Private companies also can charge more if their prisons reach a high occupancy, under the reasoning that it costs more to house more inmates. In the contract that CCA signed with Silverdale, the price paid per inmate per day went from $21 to $24 if the prison reached capacity.[16] CCA therefore crammed as many extra inmates into the facility as possible since it received more money per prisoner if the prison became overcrowded.

Another advantage for private prison companies is that they can easily move inmates between different facilities. If one prison becomes overcrowded, a company can move prisoners to another facility with more room. Private prisons commonly contract with multiple states to house prisoners in one facility while government-run prisons usually must

PRISON FOR SALE

Under Governor John Kasich, Ohio became the first state to sell a public prison to a private company in 2011. The state had hoped to sell all of its five prisons, but it was unable to close the $200 million deal. It settled on selling the Lake Erie Correctional Institution to CCA for $72.7 million. CCA began operating the prison in January 2012. In 2013, a surprise inspection by the state found numerous problems at the prison. Assaults and use of force had increased, with the prison having a higher level of assaults than public prisons in Ohio. There was a high level of gang activity and drug use. The drug use was double that of public prisons. Inmates in isolation had no access to toilets or running water.

The state withheld $500,000 in payments to the company because of the prison's problems and its inadequate staffing. Many of the problems were attributed to staff members feeling unsafe, which caused a high staff turnover rate of about 20 percent per year.[17] CCA developed a plan to address many of these issues. By 2015, the state found that Lake Erie appeared to have turned around and met standards.

hold prisoners only from the government's area of authority, such as a specific state. Public facilities that house local inmates may have times of lower and higher occupancy, but they must hire guards and other personnel even when occupancy is low. Private prisons can keep their facilities full by moving prisoners.

PICK AND CHOOSE

Another way for-profit prisons save money is in choosing the type of prisoners they want to house. It is much more

Private prisons can often choose to not house prisoners who require maximum security.

expensive to house some prisoners, such as extremely violent inmates who need solitary confinement or additional guards, than to house minimum security prisoners. Contracts in Arizona state that high-risk prisoners cannot be sent to private prisons. Therefore, Arizona public prisons are seven times more likely to house a violent inmate and three times more likely to house an inmate convicted of a high-level offense than a private prison.[18]

For-profit prisons also do not commonly accept inmates with high medical costs. Some contracts include limited medical coverage, but states pay for additional costs. In Minnesota, contracts reportedly state that for-profit prisons will not house prisoners older than 60 with high medical costs.[19] These high-cost prisoners are kept in public prisons where the added cost is picked up by taxpayers.

DISCUSSION STARTERS

- Do you think it is ethically wrong to make money from running prisons?
- Do you think the way for-profit prisons charge governments a cost per inmate per day is fair?
- Are there any prison services that you believe must be handled by the government, not by private companies?

CHAPTER FOUR

PUBLIC VS. PRIVATE

With little data available on private prisons, it's difficult to compare living conditions and other elements of life in private prisons versus public prisons.

By 2015, 29 states and the federal government were using private prisons. These facilities housed 7 percent of state prisoners.[1] New Mexico and Montana led the way with approximately 40 percent of their inmates in for-profit prisons. The federal government held 18 percent of its inmates in private prisons.[2] As for-profit prisons became more prevalent in incarcerating both state and federal prisoners, some people began to question whether private prisons truly saved the government money. Researchers soon found that this question was not easy to answer.

It was difficult to compare public and private prisons for several reasons. Contracts differ between private prisons and various states or the federal government. Populations within the prisons were difficult to compare. Plus, little data was available from private prisons. Public prisons have direct oversight from the government. Their budgets are in the public record, and they regularly publish statistics on conditions at the prison. Although individual employees at a prison may be disciplined or dismissed for wrongdoing, a public prison doesn't need to fear losing money as a result of losing a contract. In contrast, a private prison can lose its contract with the government if wrongdoing is discovered.

This motivates private prisons to cover up wrongdoing because they don't want to lose money.

Private prisons and public prisons don't necessarily hold similar populations because for-profit prisons generally do not have to care for sick or otherwise costly prisoners. Low- to mid-security inmates make up 90 percent of the private prison population compared with 69 percent in public prisons.[3] Still, a study in Mississippi found that the government paid $46.50 per day for each prisoner in a private prison compared with $35.11 to $40.47 per day in a public prison.[4]

Overall, it is difficult to get data about for-profit prisons. Some information from government contracts, such as the cost per prisoner the government pays, is available. But

COMMUNITIES TAKE THE RISK

Cities or counties sign contracts with for-profit prisons to put facilities in their communities. These contracts may seem like a good deal. The community will borrow money to build the prison. The corporation will run the facility, returning part of the money it receives for leasing bed space to the community to pay off the loans.

But it is not a good deal for the community if there are not enough prisoners to fill the prison. Policies and laws concerning crime and punishment change over time, which may cause prison populations to fluctuate. Also, companies sometimes lose their contracts to house prisoners because of mismanagement or safety concerns. The large corporations can close the doors of a prison and concentrate on other facilities. However, during times when growth in the prison population slows or when a company loses a contract, communities across the country have found themselves stuck with facilities that are empty and have little use.

for-profit prisons do not disclose their internal financial data, such as what they spend on food or salaries, to the public. Transparency laws do not apply to private companies as they do to public facilities. Only a few states, such as Connecticut, Florida, and South Carolina, include private prisons under state public record laws. News reporters and government officials can be barred from visiting private prisons or talking to inmates. Even attorneys have been barred from visiting their clients despite the fact that people in the judicial system have a right to legal counsel. On the federal level, for-profit prisons are not subject to the US Freedom of Information Act. This law allows people to request information about a government agency or facility, such as a public prison. People may request information on the number of reports of abuse in a prison or the number of hours of solitary confinement.

Congresswoman Sheila Jackson Lee, a Democrat from Texas, introduced a bill in 2005 called the Private Prison Information Act. The bill's goal was to make private prisons transparent so that costs and conditions could be more easily compared with those of public prisons. Lobbyists for the for-profit prison industry have strongly opposed the bill, calling it a slippery slope to government intrusion into private business. CCA has spent at least $7 million lobbying

Congresswoman Sheila Jackson Lee introduced a bill that aimed to provide the public with more information about the costs and living conditions of private prisons.

against the Private Prison Information Act since 2014.[5] As of 2018, the bill had not passed.

INCONCLUSIVE

Despite the lack of data from private prisons, studies have been done on the cost-effectiveness of governments using for-profit prisons instead of public prisons. In 2003, researchers conducted a national survey of administrators of private prison contracts. Administrators reported that three private prisons were meeting the requirements of their contracts, such as staffing and services. Ten were failing to meet requirements. They also reported that ten private prisons provided better quality of service than similar public prisons in several areas such as security, inmate educational services, and inmate health care. Twelve private facilities provided poorer quality of service than public prisons.[6]

In 2006, the federal Government Accountability Office (GAO) did a study of public and private prisons in Texas, California, Tennessee, New Mexico, and Washington. The study concluded that there was no evidence of cost difference. It also noted that there was not enough data available to make a clear determination of costs.[7]

A 2010 report by Arizona's Office of the Auditor General found that private prisons in the state were more expensive than public prisons. After adjusting for expenses to the state government such as medical care, the auditor found that for minimum-security prisoners, the cost was $46.81 per day in public facilities and $47.14 per day in private prisons. At medium-security prisons, public facilities paid a rate of $48.13, compared with $55.89 at private prisons.[8]

In 2011, an Arizona Department of Corrections report comparing private and public

CONVICT LABOR

Some for-profit companies make money off of inmates. As of 2018, 37 states allowed private corporations to use convict labor. This is causing a gradual labor shift to inexpensive prison labor. One American company closed a factory in Mexico and opened a replacement facility in San Quentin, California, so that it could make its products using convict labor. Another company in Texas fired 150 workers and replaced them with convict labor. In state prisons, inmates usually earn minimum wage. In private prisons, prisoners earn as little as 17 cents per hour.

prisons in the state noted that costs for prisoners of the same level were about equal, although one of the private prisons had lower quality of service.[9] Despite these findings, the state of Arizona has expanded its private prison system. A new contract in 2018 planned to bring 1,200 prisoners transferred from Puerto Rico to facilities run by CoreCivic in Arizona.

Some estimates are much more extreme. According to the *New York Times*, private prisons may cost up to $1,600 more per inmate per year than public prisons. Plus, there are many costs for governments using private prisons that are not included in the documented cost per inmate. States may have to pay for transportation of prisoners to and from out-of-state facilities. For Hawaii, which houses many of its inmates in private prisons on the US mainland, this is a significant cost. In 2009, Hawaii paid $1,506,144 to transport prisoners.[10]

Contracts may also require the government to pick up other costs. Per a 2010 agreement, the federal Immigration and Customs Enforcement agency (ICE) pays $1 a day to reimburse a for-profit detention center for wages paid to immigrant detainees working at the facility mopping floors or folding laundry. The corporation gets free labor while the taxpayers pay.

Some studies have concluded that private prisons save the government money. However, many of these have been debunked. One such study, conducted in the 1990s by a professor at the University of Florida, was discounted after it was revealed he had received millions of dollars from the for-profit prison industry. Other studies favorable to the industry by Vanderbilt University in 2008 and nonprofit organization The Reason Foundation in 2009 have also been revealed to have accepted corporate money.[11] A study in 2013 by professors at Temple University found a 14 percent cost savings for private prisons over public prisons. However, Temple withdrew any connection to the study after it was revealed that the study was funded by for-profit prison companies.

THE OBAMA POLICY

In 2016, the Federal Bureau of Prisons (BOP) conducted a study of safety and security, comparing private prisons with public prisons run by the BOP. BOP prisons were found to have more incidents of inmates testing positive for drug use. They also had more allegations of sexual misconduct by both staff and inmates. But private prisons had more assaults by inmates, more uses of force by correctional officers, more lockdowns to search for contraband or for disciplinary reasons, and more incidents of finding contraband items.

Due to inconclusive results on cost savings and concerns about security and safety, President Barack Obama's administration decided to phase out the use of private companies operating BOP prisons. In 2016, Deputy Attorney General Sally Yates announced that the use of private companies would be phased out over several years, saying:

> *Private prisons served an important role during a difficult period, but time has shown that they compare poorly to our own [bureau] facilities. They simply do not provide the same level of*

In 2016, Deputy Attorney General Sally Yates announced the federal government would phase out its use of private prisons. This decision was later reversed by the Trump administration.

correctional services, programs, and resources; they do not save substantially on costs; and as noted in a recent report by the Department's Office of Inspector General, they do not maintain the same level of safety and security.[12]

Under President Donald Trump, the move to phase out private prisons for federal inmates was reversed in February 2017. Attorney General Jeff Sessions said that Obama's decision had "changed longstanding policy and practice."[13]

REDUCING RECIDIVISM IN PENNSYLVANIA

Since 2013, Pennsylvania has contracted with private operators of community correction centers, or halfway houses that help transition prisoners back into society. The amount of money each center earns is determined by how well the facility reduces recidivism as well as how many beds are filled. The goal is to encourage private companies to invest in the training and counseling that their residents need to be successful in the community. Before the new contracts were implemented, 60 percent of people in the centers were arrested again after release. After two years of using the pay-for-performance contracts, that rate was cut in half.[14]

OTHER COUNTRIES

The United States is not the only country that contracts with private companies to run prisons. Private corporations operate prisons in many other countries including the United Kingdom, South Africa, New Zealand, and Australia. As questions arise about using for-profit prison companies, some governments are experimenting with alternative economic incentives to improve private prisons. The United Kingdom started using what are known as pay-for-performance contracts. These contracts connect the money paid to for-profit prisons with their prisoners' outcomes after being released. This has resulted in decreases in recidivism for convicts held in those prisons. Recidivism is when a person returns to criminal activities after being released from prison.

The Auckland South Correctional Facility in New Zealand is a private facility that was built to achieve positive results for prisoners. Inmates gradually work their way up to less-restrictive environments, have access to computers, and can meet with family members in private rooms. The new prison has resulted in a 10 percent reduction in recidivism.[15] These models have been used in the United States as well, but to a lesser degree.

DISCUSSION STARTERS

- Why do you think different studies of one topic, such as private prisons vs. public prisons, can provide several different results?
- Do you believe that private prisons save taxpayers money? Why or why not?
- Do you agree with President Trump's decision to reverse the policy to eliminate private prisons begun by President Obama?

THE SAGA OF
LITTLEFIELD, TEXAS

In 2000, Littlefield, Texas, borrowed $10 million for the GEO Group to build the Bill Clayton Detention Center, a state prison for juveniles. In 2003, the Texas legislature decided to remove juveniles from the facility, and GEO used the prison to house adult prisoners.

In 2009, after an audit showed mismanagement and after an inmate committed suicide following a year in solitary confinement at the prison, GEO Group lost contracts to hold prisoners from Idaho and Wyoming. With too few prisoners to make a profit, GEO closed the Littlefield facility. The city of Littlefield was left with a debt of $11 million, no prison revenue, and payments of $65,000 a month.[16] In 2011, Littlefield unsuccessfully tried to auction off the building. In 2014, Littlefield tried to contract

In 2016, the Bill Clayton facility in Littlefield, Texas, operated as a civil commitment program for sexual offenders.

with ICE to house immigrant families and children at the facility, but the contract went to other facilities instead.

In 2015, Correct Care Recovery Solutions, a spin-off of GEO Group, signed a $24 million contract to reopen the Bill Clayton facility as a civil commitment program for sexual offenders. A civil commitment program holds people who have served their sentences for a crime but are legally considered too dangerous to release into the public. In 2018, the *Texas Observer* newspaper reported inhumane treatment at the Bill Clayton facility. In addition, the facility took one-third of any money or gifts the residents received from family or friends to help pay for their treatment.

TEXAS CIVIL COMMITMENT CENTER

BILL CLAYTON FACILITY

LITTLEFIELD, TEXAS
2600 SOUTH SUNSET AVENUE

CHAPTER FIVE

INMATE CARE

Although living conditions vary at both public and private prisons, these facilities overall are known for being overcrowded.

P risons have never been known as pleasant places. Many public prisons have become notorious for poor sanitary conditions, overcrowding, and violence. For-profit prisons, even though they house mostly offenders convicted of nonviolent crimes, have faced similar problems.

There are dozens of reports of prisons providing inadequate care. In 2014, facilities in Mississippi run by Management and Training Corporation (MTC) faced lawsuits over reportedly "barbaric" conditions in a prison where mentally ill prisoners were beaten and exploited by gangs.[1] CCA opened the Northeast Ohio Correctional facility in Youngstown in 1999. Within 14 months, the prison had 13 stabbings, two murders, and six escapes. The city sued CCA for not meeting security requirements. CCA closed the prison, deciding it was no longer making a profit. In 2014, an ACLU report found that private prisons would put prisoners in solitary confinement, isolating them for up to 23 hours a day, after the prisoners filed complaints or, in one case, even when a prisoner asked for new shoes. They also used solitary confinement beds because no other beds were available.[2]

Private prisons are monitored by state authorities, but the amount of monitoring and the independence of the monitors vary by state. Even when contract

Inmates in solitary confinement are kept alone in small cells.

monitors—third-party monitors who aren't employees of the state or the prison—recommend fines for contract violations, the fines are often later reduced or not charged at all. Recommendations to close facilities are at times ignored.

Florida has full-time prison monitors. Yet, in 2017, Florida representative David Richardson visited Gadsden Correction Facility, a women's prison operated by MTC, and found abusive living conditions. Rooms were heated to only 55 degrees Fahrenheit (13°C), there was no hot water, and sick prisoners were going without health care. As a result of Richardson's report, the warden of the prison resigned.

SAFETY

Private prisons almost exclusively hold minimum- and medium-security prisoners. Private prisons usually do not disclose data on how often their prisoners attack other prisoners or prison staff. A 2005 BOP report stated that

WOMEN IN PRIVATE PRISONS

Since 1978, the rate at which women are incarcerated has grown faster than the incarceration rate for men. In 2017, 219,000 women were incarcerated in the United States. Unlike men, who are twice as likely to be held in prisons than in jails, about one-half of the country's incarcerated women are held in jails. Sixty percent of women in jails have not been convicted of a crime.[4] They are awaiting trial. Incarcerated women have a lower average income than incarcerated men, and more women are financially responsible for children. So, jailed men tend to be more able than jailed women to pay bail to be released.

For the half of incarcerated women who are in private prisons, conditions are often harsh. Gadsden Correctional Facility, the largest women's facility in Florida, is run by MTC. Recent reports by Florida congressman David Richardson have found significant health and safety problems. Many of the women lived for months without hot water or sufficient heat. Inmates were not provided adequate dental care. Prisoners also reported that they faced retaliation, such as loss of recreation time, if they spoke up about any problems at the prison.

being an inmate at a private prison seemed to reduce the probability of violent behavior. However, several other studies have shown that violence is greater in private prisons than in public ones. A 2001 Bureau of Justice Assistance report found that private prisons reported 50 percent more prisoner-on-prisoner and prisoner-on-staff assaults than public prisons with the same security levels.[3]

Much of the violence in private prisons can be attributed to inadequate staffing. Private prisons have fewer experienced correctional officers. Training for new officers may be only a few weeks, and employee turnover in private prisons is more than three times greater than in public prisons. At times, staffing waivers issued by the government allow private prisons to have less staff than public prisons. Private prison staffing may be as low as one officer per 120 prisoners.[5] The national average for state prisons was approximately one officer per six prisoners in 2010.

HEALTH CARE

In the 1976 Supreme Court case *Estelle v. Gamble*, the court ruled that it is the responsibility of prisons to provide health care for inmates, whether the person has an emergency medical situation or a chronic health problem such as cancer. Still, people in prisons often have limited access to health care, including prescription medications. A survey conducted by the National Institutes of Health concluded that both physical and mental health care in prisons was inadequate.

Today, many private and public prisons opt to contract inmate health care to for-profit companies such as Corizon, which specializes in prison health care. In some states, especially those where the contracts are closely monitored, Corizon has done well. But in other states, the company has faced many lawsuits. Corizon received $3 million in fines in Arizona for understaffing nurses and doctors. But this is a small amount compared with the $150 million the company makes each year under its contract with the state.[6] The company generally faces the same criticism as for-profit prisons for prioritizing money ahead of inmate care.

After hiring staff, health care is often the second-most expensive cost for a prison. For-profit prisons aim to keep costs low, and health care is one place this can happen. These private companies do not reveal what they spend on health care. But approximately 15 percent of lawsuits filed against CCA by inmates were for inadequate health care.[7]

Prisons operated by the Federal Bureau of Prisons must follow different standards than private prisons. BOP facilities have strict guidelines for health care. These standards are often relaxed when the government contracts to private companies. A Department of Justice report said when deaths occurred in private prisons due to medical negligence, the BOP had no way to force companies to fix the problems.

Private prisons often use medical personnel with low-level training, such as nurses with about a year of training. These nurses are often required to do medical work outside the scope of their training. Doctors reported

PRISON RIOTS FOR HEALTH CARE

Lack of proper health care can essentially be a death sentence. Inmates in private prisons have rioted over lack of adequate health care. In 2012, Adams County Correctional Center in Mississippi had a riot that killed a prison guard and left 20 other people injured. Previously, five people had died in the facility due to inadequate medical care.

that 911 calls were discouraged at private prisons because they were too expensive.

EDUCATION AND JOB TRAINING

Ideally, people who are released from prison should not return. However, the National Institute of Justice reports that 75 percent of people who leave prisons return within five years.[8] Educational opportunities can decrease this recidivism. About 40 percent of state inmates and 27 percent of federal inmates do not have a high school diploma.[9] A 2014 study by the Rand Corporation found that offering classes in prisons reduced recidivism by 13 percent and increased the chance of inmates finding jobs after leaving prison by 13 percent.[10]

Not all public prisons offer education. Among state prisons, 84 percent offer high school classes, and 27 percent offer college courses.[11] There is little data on what is offered at private prisons. A study in Mississippi indicated that public and private prisons in that state averaged close to an equal number of seats for career training programs, although the quality of the programs could not be compared.

A study of private and public prisons in Minnesota also showed that both systems offered education programs.

But the quality of the programs was substantially different. Public prisons were more likely to offer full-time general education classes. In addition, public prisons hired certified teachers and were required to follow state mandates for education. CCA set the rules for private prison education, and only half of the teachers were certified. Between 1997 and 1998, the rate of GEDs earned at public prisons was 74 per 1,000 inmates, while at private prisons it was 55 per 1,000 inmates.

The study's look at job training offered at prisons in Minnesota showed similar results. Inmates at public prisons were likely to spend more time in job training. Fifty-three percent of inmates in public prisons were satisfied with the training compared with 23 percent at the private prisons.[12]

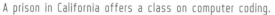
A prison in California offers a class on computer coding.

The public programs, run through contracts with state colleges and universities, allowed inmates to earn state certifications or transferable college credits. The private programs did not offer that. In federal prisons, almost all public prisons offer job training, compared with only 44 percent of private prisons.[13]

RECIDIVISM

Recidivism rates are calculated by the rearrest, reconviction, and return to prison of a person who has been released. In the United States, recidivism rates are high. A 2018 Bureau of Justice Statistics report found that 68 percent of released state prisoners were arrested within three years, 79 percent within six years, and 83 percent within nine years.[14]

Recidivism may depend on factors such as the prisoner's ability to get a job, find housing, or receive counseling and substance abuse treatment. It may also depend on the prisoner's support network. Inmates in private prisons who are moved thousands of miles away from family to fill empty beds may have more difficulty maintaining ties to their family and community. In 2013, more than 10,500 prisoners were housed in out-of-state private prisons.[15]

Recidivism is another factor that is hard to compare between public and private prisons. A 2003 Yale University study on Florida prisons found that private prisons had significantly higher recidivism rates. However, a 2005 report by the Florida Department of Corrections, Florida State University, and Florida's Correctional Privatization Commission found almost no difference in recidivism rates at private and public prisons.

In 2008, a study of Oklahoma inmates found that recidivism rates were significantly higher at private prisons. It also found that when prisoners were confined in private prisons for longer amounts of time, they had higher chances of recidivism. The study concluded that prisoners held in private prisons were 16.7 percent more likely to return to prison. A study in 2013 by the Minnesota Department of Corrections also found that prisoners in private prisons were more likely to have higher recidivism rates. The study attributed the higher rates to fewer visitations and fewer rehabilitation programs at for-profit prisons. Other research shows that states with the highest percentages of private prison beds—such as New Mexico, Alaska, Hawaii, and Vermont—also have some of the highest three-year recidivism rates.

Some government officials believe work and education programs will reduce recidivism rates. These Nevada prisoners are participating in a gardening program as part of their prison's efforts to reduce recidivism.

There is no clear evidence that private prisons provide the same quality of care as public prisons. There is evidence that cost-cutting measures in education and health care are problems in many private prisons. However, even with research indicating that private prisons may not be the best choice for prisoners' well-being or for taxpayers' wallets, many lawmakers still choose to contract with for-profit prisons. The reasons behind these decisions may vary, but they often have to do with money and politics.

DISCUSSION STARTERS

- What do you believe is the most important factor in determining whether a person returns to prison after being released?
- Do you think prisons should be primarily for punishment or rehabilitation? Why?
- Do you think the government should set minimum requirements for the training of guards and medical personnel at private prisons?

CHAPTER SIX

PRISONS AND POLITICS

Some people support prisons as a way to provide job
opportunities, such as corrections officer jobs, in rural areas.

F or politicians, the issue of prisons is a tricky one. Taxpayers often elect officials who promise to be tough on crime. But voters do not want their tax dollars spent on building new prisons. Shifting the burden of building new facilities to for-profit companies seems like a good solution.

New prisons, which are primarily built in rural areas, can also be a political win for politicians who get a facility built in their district. Private prisons offer jobs in rural areas where unemployment is high. In addition, they offer training and experience in law enforcement. A prison can also be a boon to other businesses in the community, such as laundromats, that can offer services to the prison. They can also benefit restaurants and hotels that serve people coming to visit prisoners.

LOBBYING

For private prisons to thrive, there must be states that are willing to turn over inmates to private companies as well as laws that keep the number of prisoners high. Private prison companies contribute generously to political candidates who serve their interests. For-profit prison companies contributed $1.6 million to candidates they felt would further their interests during the 2016 federal election cycle.[1] These companies' political interests might include endorsing laws that increase the prison population or laws that make doing business with for-profit companies easier.

For-profit prisons, like other industries, also hire lobbyists to work with government leaders to promote their industry. Lobbyists meet with government officials, propose new laws, and do other work that benefits the industry they represent. Between 2002 and 2012, CCA spent $17 million on lobbying. GEO spent $2.5 million from 2004 to 2012.[2] These large amounts of money for elections and lobbying can at times lead to corruption.

The for-profit prison industry is also served by state laws that make it easier for private prisons to operate. In Florida, GEO Group contributed $1.5 million in campaign contributions to state officials from 2003 to 2010. Florida law requires that a certain number of prisons be operated by private companies. Some

LOBBYISTS IN THE UNITED STATES

The term *lobbying* comes from the place—the lobby—where people at one time tried to talk to legislators. There is no education or licensing requirement to become a lobbyist, although most lobbyists have a college degree. Lobbyists are required to register with the federal or state government where they plan to lobby, and companies are required to disclose people they pay to be lobbyists. Laws restrict lobbyists from paying more than $50 for a gift to a politician. Laws also restrict the time legislators must wait before they become lobbyists after leaving office. In 2017, there were 11,529 registered lobbyists in the United States.[3]

Florida state government officials are trying to make more prisons privately run.

There is often a revolving door of relationships among lobbyists, high-level government employees involved in running prisons, and top jobs at private prisons. Lobbyists are often people who once worked in government. They have inside information about government policy and important contacts with government officials. In August 2016, GEO hired two lobbyists who had previously worked as aides to Attorney General Jeff Sessions when he was a US senator. Additionally, officials from for-profit prison corporations are sometimes appointed to government positions. In Ohio, Governor John Kasich appointed a former employee of CCA as director of Ohio's Department of Corrections.

GERRYMANDERING AND PRISONS

Under the US Constitution, the federal government takes a census of the total population of the country every ten years. The total population of each state is used to apportion the number of representatives in the House of Representatives that each state receives. States with large populations receive larger shares of the 435 representatives in the House. As people move around within the United States or

Gerrymandering often results in oddly shaped voting districts.

immigrate from outside the United States, the number of representatives a state receives may change after the census.

Within states, the census numbers are used to draw districts that vote for House representatives and state offices. Under the Fourteenth Amendment to the Constitution, the Supreme Court has ruled that districts must contain approximately equal numbers of people so that citizens of one district do not have more representation than another. The party in power after a census usually gets to redraw the district lines using the new population numbers.

Political parties often try to draw district lines that give their party an advantage in the next election. This process is called gerrymandering. They may try to distribute a region that contains a majority of an opposing party into several districts so that the opposing party becomes a minority in each district. Or they may try to group voters from their own party who are scattered across a region into one district.

Another way to gerrymander a district is to use a prison. The US Census counts inmates of a prison as part of the local population. However, in most states, convicted felons can't vote. Therefore, voters are overrepresented in districts with a prison. In the 2002 city council wards in Anamosa, Iowa, Ward 2 had approximately 1,300 prisoners and only 58 eligible voters. This gave Ward 2 voters 25 times more voting influence than voters in other wards.[4]

New district lines proposed in Wyoming in 2012 put two state senators of the same political party in the same district. To avoid having these two run against each other for reelection, the district lines were moved 17 miles (27 km), moving a prison from one district to another. This shifted the voting populations in a way that allowed the senators to win their elections in their own districts.

Since most new prisons are built in rural areas, and most of those incarcerated are from urban areas, prison gerrymandering creates a higher population, and therefore more voting power, in rural areas. And because many people of color from cities are incarcerated in majority-white rural areas, these white districts benefit from their incarceration by getting more voting power through gerrymandering.

In the 1980s, as the result of a lawsuit, Maryland was court-ordered to create a majority-black district. The goal was to avoid redistricting that kept black voters from electing a black candidate. Still, no black candidate was elected. The

When a person votes in a district that has fewer eligible voters than another, the vote will carry more weight. Political parties use this to their advantage by gerrymandering, or redrawing voting districts to include more eligible voters of their own party, offset by prison populations.

PRISON GERRYMANDERING

DISTRICT 1

100
VOTERS

DISTRICT 2

75
VOTERS

PRISON WITH 25 INMATES

District 1 has 100 people living in it. All are eligible to vote. They have the voting power to elect one representative.

District 2 has 100 people living in it too. But 25 are prison inmates who are not eligible to vote. The 75 voters in this district together have equal voting power to the 100 voters in District 1.

new district had a prison. Although the inmates contributed to the black population of the district, they could not vote. So, white voters still elected white candidates. In 2010, Maryland passed the No Representation Without Population Act, which requires inmates to be counted in their home district rather than the prison district.

GERRYMANDERING REFORM

When politicians depend on prisons in their districts, whether through gerrymandering or economics, it may sway their votes on prison reform. Districts given more power through gerrymandering may tend to vote for politicians who will help them retain that power by voting for tough-on-crime laws or for building new prisons.

In the 2000s, both political parties supported lessening the Rockefeller Laws in New York. The New York state senate took the matter under consideration, but two important senators opposed it. One was Dale Volker, head

A WINNER WITH TWO VOTES

In 2005, Danny Young set a record for the fewest votes cast to win an election. Young got a total of two votes and won a city council seat in Anamosa, Iowa. The town, with a population of 5,000, including a prison, was divided into four wards. There were 1,400 people in Young's ward, but 1,300 were prisoners who couldn't vote. Voter turnout was low, and Young's opponent got only one vote. When asked if he felt he represented the prisoners, Young replied, "They don't vote, so, I guess, not really."[5]

of the committee that decides where to build new prisons. The other was the head of the Crime Committee, Michael Nozzolio. Both had prisons in their districts, but both denied this had anything to do with their opposition. Rebecca Thorpe, a political scientist, did a study on opposition to drug reform laws in California. She found that districts with prisons were more likely to oppose reforming marijuana laws than districts without prisons. A district with two prisons, especially in a rural area, was more likely to oppose reforming the laws than a district with one prison. Prisoners who do not have the right to vote and who are incarcerated far from their homes are effectively denied representation. Representatives from districts with prisons often ignore the

RIGHT TO VOTE

Mass incarceration, enabled by for-profit prisons, has affected voting in the United States. About six million people can't vote due to felony convictions. About one-half of these people have completed their sentences, one-quarter are under probation or parole, and one-quarter are still in prison.[6] The US Constitution gives people the right to vote, and that right cannot be denied based on race or gender. However, no federal law says whether people convicted of a felony have the right to vote. Whether a felon has the right to vote is decided in each state. Most people convicted of a felony lose the right to vote while they are in prison. Only two states, Maine and Vermont, allow felons to vote while they are incarcerated. Fourteen states and the District of Columbia allow felons to vote automatically once they are no longer incarcerated. Twenty-two states allow felons to vote once they are no longer incarcerated, under parole, or on probation, and once they have paid fees or fines associated with their convictions. In 12 states, the right to vote is permanently lost with convictions of certain crimes, and a waiting period or governor's pardon is required to restore voting rights.

People who believe gerrymandering is unfair protest publicly against it.

people incarcerated there. Volker said that his attention goes to the people who work at the prison, not the prisoners.

In 2016, the Supreme Court ruled in *Evenwel v. Abbott* that states may draw district lines based on total population, including prisoners, rather than voting population. However, many states have passed their own laws that require prisoners to be counted at their residence before incarceration rather than at the prison. This not only discourages states from using prisons as political tools but also increases government spending in districts where inmates and their families live.

In 2015, Congress proposed the Fairness in Incarcerated Representation Act to require that inmates be counted in the US Census at the location of their last residence before they were convicted. Opposition pointed out that the census requires a physical presence. The proposal is similar to how US service members stationed overseas are counted. The bill did not pass. However, the census now releases a count of the prison population in time for states to redraw districts if they choose to use it.

DISCUSSION STARTERS

- Do you believe that convicted felons should lose the right to vote?
- Do you think gerrymandering is fair? What do you think would be the best way to draw voting districts?
- Do you think people or businesses should be allowed to give unlimited funds to political campaigns?

CHAPTER SEVEN

IMMIGRANT DETENTION

Due to the release of many prisoners in the late 2000s, for-profit prisons turned to immigrant detention to continue making money.

The early 1990s were growth years for the for-profit prison industry. Anticipating continued growth in the prison population, private prison companies, as well as governments, built many new prisons. Between 1984 and 2005, a new prison opened every 8.5 days.[1]

As studies revealed questionable savings to governments and reports came out about unsafe and poor conditions in private prisons, more governments began to question whether for-profit prisons saved money or provided adequate living conditions. A few states banned private prisons. Illinois banned private state prisons in 1990, and the state of New York later followed suit.

Worse yet for a business that depended on filling beds with prisoners, the prison population began to drop. The country's high increase in incarcerations had stopped by 2000, and the prison population stabilized by 2008. After that, the prison population began to slowly go down. As states began to cancel contracts, CCA's stock price dropped 93 percent from 1998 to 2000. GEO Group's stock went down by two-thirds in that same time frame.[2] For-profit prison companies had to find another way to make money, so they turned to providing facilities for immigrant detention.

THE FEDERAL INCARCERATION SYSTEM

The federal government has a multitiered system of incarceration. The BOP has prisons that house prisoners, primarily US citizens, who have been convicted of federal crimes. They also have low-security prisons called Criminal Alien Requirement (CAR) prisons, which mainly hold undocumented immigrants who have been convicted of minor drug crimes or immigration violations and are awaiting deportation once their sentence is served.

Many immigrant detention centers, which may also be called residential centers, are operated through agreements between private companies and the federal government.

CAR prisons were created in response to a 2005 government policy, Operation Streamline, to expedite the criminal prosecution of immigrants caught at the border. CAR facilities do not have to offer programs for drug rehabilitation, mental health treatment, or education, all of which are mandated for regular federal prisons. It is assumed that most people in CAR prisons are detained for short periods of time and will most likely not be returning to society in the United States because they will be deported. CAR prisons are run almost exclusively by private companies.

The third tier of incarceration consists of immigrant detention centers. Immigrant detention centers are technically not prisons because they house people who have not been convicted of a crime. Instead of being part of the BOP, these centers are under the control of ICE. Undocumented immigrants are held against their will in these facilities as they wait for the federal government to determine whether they may stay in the country. ICE Enforcement and Removal Operations (ERO) manages these centers. The federal Department of Health and Human Services' Office of Refugee Resettlement is responsible for unaccompanied immigrant children. These children are held in separate detention centers.

MORE DETENTION CENTERS

The number of CAR facilities and detention centers grew quickly after 2005. In 2008, thousands of immigrants fleeing gangs and drug cartels in Central America began arriving at the southern border of the United States. The government expanded the detention of mothers and children by 4,000 percent.[3] In 2009, Congress mandated that at least 33,400 detention center beds should be available to ICE whether the agency needed them or not. That mandate was increased to 34,000 beds in 2011.[4]

The growth in for-profit prison corporations moved from working with state and local governments to working more with the federal government. Since 2000, the number of people in private prisons has increased 47 percent, compared with an overall rise in the prison population of 9 percent. The federal system has increased its use of private prisons by 120 percent since 2000.[5]

Most of this growth was because of increased immigrant detention. From 1995 to 2013, the

WHAT IS ICE?

Immigration and Customs Enforcement (ICE) was formed in 2003 under the new Department of Homeland Security. The old Immigration and Naturalization Service (INS) was closed, and the administration of immigrant applications and other documents was turned over to the US Bureau of Citizenship and Immigration Services. ICE is tasked with enforcing immigration laws.

number of people kept in ICE detention centers rose from 85,000 to 440,557. More people went through the immigrant detention system than through federal prisons.[6] In 2017, 71 percent of immigrants detained were in private prisons.[7]

CCA and GEO Group opened 72 percent of the new ICE detention beds. Between October 2013 and June 2014, 39,000 adults with children were detained at the border.[8] The money that ICE paid to CCA to hold immigrant detainees doubled from 2014 to 2015. At the same time, CCA's income from BOP to hold convicted inmates decreased from 13 percent to 9 percent of its total revenue.[9] This shows that a larger number of undocumented immigrants detained in 2015 had not been convicted of a crime.

WILLACY COUNTY TRIES AGAIN

In 2006, MTC opened the Willacy County Regional Detention Center in Texas as a federal detention center for immigrants awaiting deportation or court decisions. Due to widespread abuse at the Willacy Detention Center, ICE did not renew its contract with MTC in 2011. Shortly after, MTC acquired a contract with the Bureau of Prisons and reopened the facility as a Criminal Alien Requirement (CAR) prison. The facility became the Willacy County Correctional Center. It housed 2,700 immigrant prisoners, many of whom were convicted of drug-related crimes or reentering the United States after being deported.[10] The prison sentence for illegal reentry could be from two to 20 years. Willacy had been hastily constructed and housed inmates in Kevlar tents behind barbed wire fences in unsanitary and crowded conditions. In 2015, a riot at the prison caused severe damage, and the facility was closed. Willacy County sued MTC for mismanagement. In June 2017, ICE, Willacy County, and MTC signed a new agreement to open a 1,000-bed facility to house immigrant detainees. Many people protested the decision, citing concerns about abuse and human rights. But supporters of the facility noted that it serves as a significant job provider in the county.

IMMIGRANT CRACKDOWN

After the election of President Trump, ICE expanded its efforts away from the border, further into the United States. The agency received $2.5 billion to hold up to 47,000 immigrants. In the first nine months of 2017, ICE arrests increased 42 percent from the previous year.[11] In February 2017, the US Supreme Court ruled that undocumented immigrants do not have a right to bond hearings, as citizens do. This meant that these people could be detained indefinitely while waiting for the courts to decide whether they would be deported.

These new policies were a boon for private prisons. After Trump's election, the stock for CoreCivic (formerly known as CCA) rose 81 percent in less than a year. GEO Group received a $457 million contract to build and run a 1,000-bed immigrant detention center outside of

STATE LAW TARGETING IMMIGRANTS

In 2010, Arizona passed a law that required police officers to demand proof of legal residency from anyone stopped for any reason if an officer suspected that the person was an undocumented immigrant. Most of the lawmakers who cosponsored the bill had received donations from for-profit prison companies. Immigrant rights groups sued the state for racial profiling and other civil rights violations. They claimed officers were more likely to demand proof of residency from people of color than from white people. After six years, the state settled the lawsuits by agreeing not to enforce most provisions of the bill, including the part that demands officers request proof of residency.

Houston, Texas. GEO's stock increased 63 percent in the 11 months after Trump's election.[12]

PROTECTING IMMIGRANTS

The massive growth in detained immigrants resulted in overcrowding in the detention centers, even as private companies built more facilities. Private companies found places ranging from old hotels to groups of tents and rented them to the federal government to hold immigrant detainees.

In 2014, the ACLU released a report of a four-year investigation into four CAR prisons in Texas. Investigators "found pervasive and disturbing patterns of neglect and abuse of the prisoners."[13] Among complaints were overuse of solitary confinement, prisoners crammed into hallways for sleeping quarters, and inadequate health care.

Still, congressional bills to protect detained immigrants stalled. As of 2018, Congress had not passed the Dignity for Detained Immigrants Act, which would establish enforceable standards for immigration centers including unannounced visits by the inspector general of Homeland Security, media access, higher fines for noncompliance, and disclosure requirements. The Private Prison Information Act, which would have made for-profit prisons subject to Freedom of Information Act (FOIA) requests, also did not pass Congress. However, in October 2017, the Supreme Court ruled against CoreCivic and GEO Group when they tried to block FOIA requests to release information from the federal government about for-profit contracts.

SEPARATING FAMILIES

In April 2018, President Trump announced a new policy of "zero tolerance" for immigrants crossing the border.[14] The United States would prosecute all immigrants crossing the border illegally. Illegal entry into the United States is a federal misdemeanor crime. Misdemeanors are legally considered less serious than felony crimes.

The Trump administration has been criticized for allowing many immigrant children to be separated from their parents in detention centers.

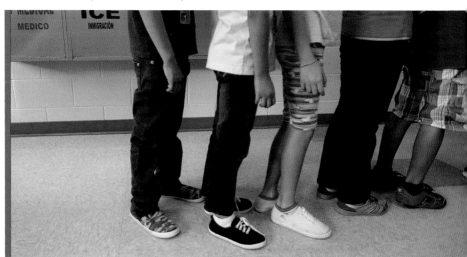

Many of the immigrants who fell under Trump's policy were families fleeing violence in Central America. The parents from these families were held in detention centers. Since minors are not allowed to be held in adult prisons, the children were taken from their parents. The Trump administration hoped that separating children from parents would deter immigrants from coming into the United States.

By May, more than 2,300 children had been separated from their parents.[15] Once separated from their parents, the children were treated as unaccompanied minors and placed into the custody of the Department of Human Services (DHS). The DHS, unprepared for the influx of minors, dispersed the children to facilities across the United States.

Media coverage and lawyers representing the immigrants brought a public outcry at the separation of children, many of them toddlers, from their parents. On June 20, Trump signed an executive order to stop the separations. On June 26, a federal judge ordered that the more than 2,500 children be reunited with their parents within 30 days.

But reuniting these families was easier said than done. ICE had turned the children over to DHS. DHS then had to find their parents—but some of these parents had been moved between different ICE facilities, and others had been deported. By mid-July, the Trump administration reported that all eligible children younger than age five had been reunited with their families. However, this amounted to only half of the detained children younger than five. The Trump administration cited safety issues, deportation of these children's parents, and other concerns as the reasons the children were ineligible to be reunited with their families. The government missed its deadline for reuniting all families. As of August 2018, hundreds of children had not been reunited with their parents.[16] This debacle has brought public attention to the plight of all immigrants detained by the United States government—almost all of whom are held in private prisons and detention centers.

DISCUSSION STARTERS

- Do you think all undocumented immigrants should be detained in detention centers, or should they be released while awaiting court dates?
- Do you think ICE's increased enforcement in 2017 and 2018 was helpful, harmful, or both?
- How has the for-profit prison industry affected immigration?

CHAPTER EIGHT

THE FUTURE OF FOR-PROFIT PRISONS

Although the US prison population has decreased since 1997, for-profit prison corporations continue to make money.

I n 1998, journalist Eric Schlosser wrote, "Three decades after the war on crime began, the United States has developed a prison-industrial complex—a set of bureaucratic, political, and economic interests that encourage increased spending on imprisonment, regardless of the actual need."[1] In other words, the increase in spending on incarceration in the United States has largely been driven not by fighting crime but by economic motivations. This was still true in 2018 as immigrant detention increased.

As of 2018, the US prison rate was the lowest since 1997, and violent crime had decreased. But the growth of for-profit prisons has created an economic incentive for incarceration. Prisons provide billions of dollars in revenue to multiple corporations. They supply jobs and revenue to poor communities, especially those in rural areas. They also put money for reelection campaigns in the pockets of politicians. Since 1989, for-profit prison corporations have spent $25 million lobbying and $10 million in political donations.[2]

Still, not all communities are convinced that private prisons are a good thing. As of 2018, Iowa joined New York and Illinois in banning private prisons. Twenty other states did not use private prisons, but the facilities were not banned by law. Eight other states reduced their use of private prisons between 2000 and 2016. As of 2018, the federal government had the largest number of inmates in private prisons.[3]

Other states are finding different ways to work with for-profit prison companies. Kansas has contracted with CoreCivic to build a 2,400-bed prison to replace Lansing Prison, which is 155 years old. CoreCivic planned to construct and maintain the building for $160 million while the state government would lease the building from CoreCivic and run the prison operations. So, the private company would become the landlord of the prison until the state paid its debt.

THE DIVESTMENT MOVEMENT

Some groups have decided to divest from private prison corporations. Much of this divestment, or removal of investment, is being done for ethical reasons. Columbia University was the first university to divest from private prisons in 2015. Students discovered that the university held approximately $8 million in CCA

STUDENT PROTEST

In February 2013, Florida Atlantic University signed an agreement with GEO Group to put the company's name on its new football stadium, home of the Florida Atlantic Owls. George Zoley, CEO of GEO Group, is an alumnus of the school. Students immediately protested having the name of a for-profit prison company displayed on their stadium. The university canceled the $6 million contract, and the university's president resigned shortly after.

stock and $2 million in stock of G4S, an international security company. They formed a group called Prison Divest, wrote a letter to the university president, and posted a recording of the letter on YouTube. Columbia decided to divest.

The University of California system divested six months later, selling its $25 million worth of investments in CCA, G4S, and GEO Group. Other student groups, including those from Northwestern University, Princeton University, Swarthmore College, and Yale University, petitioned their universities to divest. Yale student Joseph Gaylin explained: "Yale is [an] intellectual institution and leader and should not be investing in something that destroys entire populations and is used to keep people down in our society."[4]

Groups outside of universities have also decided to divest. These have included church groups such as the United Methodist pension and health plan, large corporations such as General Electric, cities including Portland, Oregon, and Berkeley, California, and even large investment companies.

NEW REVENUES

To offset the cost of prisons, governments have found other sources of revenue within the criminal justice system. Some charge for services such as probation or electronic monitoring. Some states even charge for public defenders. South Dakota charges $92 per hour. In 1974, the US Supreme Court ruled that fining prisoners for court costs, even if they don't have money to pay when they're convicted, does not violate the Fourteenth Amendment of the US Constitution, which requires equal treatment of all citizens under laws.

These new revenues gathered from outside the prison system have grown. While prison populations decline, local jail populations, which consist of people awaiting trial or serving time for minor offenses, grew by almost 20 percent between 2000 and 2014. Those detained awaiting trial accounted for 95 percent of that growth.[5]

Private prison companies have stepped into this market. In Georgia, private companies collected $100 million in

BAIL BONDS

Bail is money that a person accused of a crime gives the court so that he or she can go home instead of remaining in jail while awaiting trial. In a standard bail agreement, the money is returned to the person once his or her court case has concluded. The median bail amount for a felony arrest is $10,000. Many people don't have that kind of money, and about 500,000 people are in jail awaiting court dates. People who can't afford bail can get the money from private bail-bond companies. These companies loan people bail money, but once the person's court case has concluded and he or she is repaid, his or her bail-bond company will charge a fee equal to 10 percent of the bail amount. Bail-bond companies keep this money regardless of whether people are innocent or guilty. In Maryland alone, people who were accused of crimes and were later acquitted spent $75 million on nonrefundable bail over five years. The bail-bond industry makes about $2 billion in profit per year. The United States and the Philippines are the only countries that allow private bail companies.[6]

Electronic monitoring bracelets are used to give certain inmates the option of being released from jail while still being monitored by criminal justice officials. However, inmates who choose this option often have to pay fees.

fines, court costs, and restitution in 2012.[7] Even if a person is innocent of the criminal charge in his or her court case, not paying court fees is a crime. So, there is a revolving door of people being released and then rearrested for not paying fees. This mostly affects low-income people who can't afford to pay these fees. The *Tulsa World* newspaper in Oklahoma reported that 28 percent of people jailed in 2014 were arrested on debt-related reasons, up from 8 percent in 2004.[8]

THE TREATMENT INDUSTRIAL COMPLEX

Advocates for prison reform argue that money spent on building private prisons and keeping them full could be better spent on other programs for drug rehabilitation, mental health treatment, and job training. Approximately 50 percent of inmates have mental health or substance abuse problems, compared with 1 to 3 percent of the general population.[9] The companies that run for-profit prisons have listened, and they are beginning to change the focus of their businesses as prison incarceration rates go down.

The private prison industry has been skillful at remaking itself as policies change. The large companies stepped in when governments needed prison beds. They then adapted to become essential in furnishing beds for immigrant detainees. Today, as more states are considering prison reform, private companies are moving into the new market of what is known as community corrections. Community corrections are facilities for people who have served their prison sentences and are transitioning back into society. They include services such as mental health treatment, substance abuse treatment, halfway houses, and job training. Private prisons are looking to fill this need for facilities that house and rehabilitate people. GEO Group has created a new

FORENSIC COMMITMENT

Although prison populations have declined, forensic commitment has increased. Forensic commitment is when people linked to crimes are held against their will due to severe mental illness. This includes people who have been judged incompetent to stand trial because of mental illness. They are held in state hospitals until they are considered fit to stand trial, though some never make it to trial. Forensic commitment also includes people who are judged to be clinically insane at the time they committed a crime. They are sentenced to stay in state hospitals, and they may be released early if a court finds that their sanity has been restored. In 1993, states spent 10.3 percent of state psychiatric budgets on forensic patients. By 2007, that had increased to 26 percent.[18] As states have struggled to house committed mental health patients, for-profit prison companies have begun building facilities for them.

company, Correct Care Solutions, which has opened seven treatment centers. These include five mental health facilities and two civil commitment centers.

Other new revenues for private prisons are flowing from prison reforms. Private companies have stepped in to supply services for alternatives to incarceration. These include home confinement, electronic monitoring, and probation and parole services. People could be forced to choose between paying for these services themselves or spending time in jail. This saves taxpayer dollars at the expense of people accused of crimes, whether they are guilty or not.

THE FUTURE

The economic impact of incarceration is $80 billion a year. This includes the pay to prison employees plus service industries such as transportation and food.[11] For-profit prisons have about 8 to 9 percent of this business.

As of January 2018, for-profit prisons housed 126,000 federal and state prisoners.[12] This was down from the peak of the private prison population, 137,220 prisoners in 2012.[13] In a market society, money is made through supply and demand. For private prisons to make a profit, people must be incarcerated. For the companies to grow, they must increase profits each year. If there are not enough inmates, the companies will close prisons, often leaving their communities to pick up the tab.

This cycle may discourage lawmakers from reforming the prison system. It may also encourage local governments to look for more revenue to pay for the cost of incarceration. They may do this by holding people awaiting trials to keep prisons full, charging court fees, or charging high rates for using email or making phone calls in prison.

As long as laws require incarceration and other forms of confinement or monitoring, there will be a need for facilities that house convicted criminals, people awaiting trial, or undocumented immigrants awaiting processing. And as long as communities are unable or unwilling to build and maintain these facilities, it seems that for-profit companies will fill that need.

DISCUSSION STARTERS

- Would you be in favor of building a for-profit prison in your community? Why or why not?
- Do you believe that for-profit prisons are ethical?
- Do you think the United States will continue using private prisons in the future?

ESSENTIAL FACTS

SIGNIFICANT EVENTS

- The War on Drugs and harsh penalties sent the prison population soaring in the 1980s.

- The first modern for-profit prisons were established in the mid-1980s as a response to mass incarceration.

- President Obama created a policy in 2016 to gradually eliminate the use of for-profit prisons for federal prisoners.

- President Trump reversed the Obama policy in 2017 and significantly increased the number of immigrants placed in detention centers.

KEY PLAYERS

- CoreCivic (formerly known as the Corrections Corporation of America, or CCA) is the largest for-profit prison company in the United States.

- GEO Group is the second-largest for-profit prison company in the United States.

- Nelson Rockefeller, former governor of New York, introduced tough-on-crime policies in 1973.

- President Ronald Reagan fueled the War on Drugs in the 1980s, introducing policies that vastly increased the country's prison population.

- President Donald Trump increased immigration detention in 2017, and many of the detainees were placed in facilities run by for-profit companies.

IMPACT ON SOCIETY

Laws from the early 1980s and beyond have led to mass incarceration in the United States. The population of people in prisons and jails went up 500 percent from 1976 to 2016. This, in turn, has led to a rise in for-profit prisons to provide facilities to house prisoners. For-profit prisons have become a $5 billion industry. The growth of this industry has prompted some advocates to call for prison reform, seeking to spend less money on incarceration and more on rehabilitation.

QUOTE

"Three decades after the war on crime began, the United States has developed a prison-industrial complex—a set of bureaucratic, political, and economic interests that encourage increased spending on imprisonment, regardless of the actual need."

—Journalist Eric Schlosser

GLOSSARY

appeal
A request for a higher court to review the decision of a lower court.

banned
Not allowed.

bond
An amount of money accused people pay to the court to ensure they will appear at trial after being released from custody.

capacity
The total number of people for which a facility was built.

confinement
The state of being restricted to a particular space.

contraband
Items that are banned.

detainee
Someone who is being held by a government who is not accused of a crime.

detention center
A facility for holding people not accused of a crime; also a term often used for juvenile prisons.

deterrent
An action or thing that works to prevent a particular outcome.

electronic monitoring
Use of electronic bracelets, GPS, or other devices to keep track of people on parole or probation.

GED
A General Education Development certificate, which proves a person's high school–level education.

halfway house
A facility where inmates are given more freedom to work or see family as they move from prison back into society.

incarcerated
Held against one's will for committing a crime or while awaiting trial.

inconclusive
Not clearly leading to one outcome.

mandatory
Required.

parole
Early release from prison because of good behavior under the condition that good behavior continue.

probation
The release of a prisoner who remains under supervision instead of incarceration.

rehabilitate
To use education or therapy to return someone to a normal life after criminal activity or substance abuse.

restitution
Money paid for injury or loss.

truancy
Staying away from school without a good excuse.

waiver
Permission to ignore rules.

ADDITIONAL RESOURCES

SELECTED BIBLIOGRAPHY

Edelman, Peter. *Not a Crime to Be Poor*. New Press, 2017.

Eisen, Lauren-Brooke. *Inside Private Prisons*. Columbia UP, 2018.

Swygert, Dorothy R. *Silence in a Democracy: Prisons for Profit*. Rekindle the Heart, 2016.

FURTHER READINGS

Burlingame, Jeff. *Prisons*. Cavendish, 2012.

Forman, James. *Locking Up Our Own: Crime and Punishment in Black America*. Farrar, Straus and Giroux, 2017.

Harris, Duchess, and Kate Conley. *The US Prison System and Prison Life*. Abdo, 2020.

ONLINE RESOURCES

To learn more about for-profit prisons, visit **abdobooklinks.com** or scan this QR code. These links are routinely monitored and updated to provide the most current information available.

MORE INFORMATION

For more information on this subject, contact or visit the following organizations:

Abolish Private Prisons
125 N. Second St., Suite 110, Box 521
Phoenix, AZ 85004
abolishprivateprisons.org

This nonprofit organization works to raise awareness about the problems with private prisons and to abolish the private prison industry.

GEO Group
621 NW Fifty-Third St., Suite 700
Boca Raton, FL 33487
561-893-0101
geogroup.com

This is one of the largest for-profit prison companies in the United States. Its operations include management or ownership of 136 facilities.

The Marshall Project
156 W. Fifty-Sixth St., Suite 701
New York, NY 10019
212-803-5200
themarshallproject.org

This nonprofit news organization reports on the criminal justice system.

SOURCE NOTES

CHAPTER 1. KIDS FOR CASH

1. Peter Wagner and Wendy Sawyer. "Mass Incarceration: The Whole Pie 2018." *Prison Policy Initiative*, 14 Mar. 2018, prisonpolicy.org. Accessed 11 Dec. 2018.

2. Ian Ubrina and Sean D. Hamill. "Judges Plead Guilty in Scheme to Jail Youths for Profit." *New York Times*, 12 Feb. 2009, nytimes.com. Accessed 11 Dec. 2018.

3. Larry Getlen. "Corrupt 'Kids for Cash' Judge Ruined More Than 2,000 Lives." *New York Post*, 23 Feb. 2014, nypost.com. Accessed 11 Dec. 2018.

4. Getlen, "Corrupt 'Kids for Cash' Judge Ruined More Than 2,000 Lives."

5. Getlen, "Corrupt 'Kids for Cash' Judge Ruined More Than 2,000 Lives."

6. "Mother in 'Kids for Cash' Scandal Says She Got Justice." *CNN*, 15 Aug. 2011, cnn.com. Accessed 11 Dec. 2018.

7. Wagner and Sawyer, "Mass Incarceration: The Whole Pie 2018."

8. Michelle Ye Hee Lee. "Yes, U.S. Locks People Up at a Higher Rate Than Any Other Country." *Washington Post*, 7 July 2015, washingtonpost.com. Accessed 11 Dec. 2018.

9. "Notorious Private Prison Closes Today in Walnut Grove, Mississippi." *ACLU*, 15 Sept. 2016, aclu.org. Accessed 11 Dec. 2018.

CHAPTER 2. PRISONERS FOR PROFIT

1. "13th Amendment to the U.S. Constitution." *Library of Congress*, n.d., guides.loc.gov. Accessed 11 Dec. 2018.

2. Lauren-Brooke Eisen. *Inside Private Prisons*. Columbia UP, 2017. 49.

3. Eisen, *Inside Private Prisons*, 49.

4. Eisen, *Inside Private Prisons*, 49.

5. Nancy Gertner and Chiraag Bains. "Mandatory Minimum Sentences Are Cruel and Ineffective. Sessions Wants Them Back." *Washington Post*, 15 May 2017, washingtonpost.com. Accessed 11 Dec. 2018.

6. Gertner and Bains, "Mandatory Minimum Sentences Are Cruel and Ineffective."

7. "The Punishing Decade: Prison and Jail Estimates at the Millennium." *Justice Policy Institute*, May 2000, justicepolicy.org. Accessed 11 Dec. 2018.

8. Megan Mumford, Diane Whitmore Schanzenbach, and Ryan Nunn. "The Economics of Private Prisons." *Hamilton Project*, n.d., brookings.edu. Accessed 11 Dec. 2018.

9. Eric Schlosser. "The Prison-Industrial Complex." *Atlantic*, Dec. 1998, theatlantic.com. Accessed 11 Dec. 2018.

10. Stanton P. Field and Roger D. Thompson. "Prison Overcrowding: The Experience in Tennessee." *American Journal of Criminal Justice*, vol. 11, issue 1, 95–102.

CHAPTER 3. THE RETURN OF PRIVATE PRISONS

1. "Prisons for Profit: Incarceration for Sale." *American Bar Association*, 7 Mar. 2012, americanbar.org. Accessed 11 Dec. 2018.

2. Jordan King and Anthony Chen. "Private Prisons: An Evaluation of Economic and Ethical Implications." *Penn Wharton Public Policy Initiative*, 25 Jan. 2018, publicpolicy.wharton.upenn.edu. Accessed 11 Dec. 2018.

3. "CoreCivic Inc. Revenue, Profits." *Amigobulls*, 10 Dec. 2018, amigobulls.com. Accessed 11 Dec. 2018.

4. Shane Bauer. "My Four Months as a Private Prison Guard." *Mother Jones*, July/Aug. 2016, motherjones.com. Accessed 11 Dec. 2018.

5. "GEO Group Revenue, Profits." *Amigobulls*, 10 Dec. 2018, amigobulls.com. Accessed 11 Dec. 2018.

6. David Gambacorta. "Dead Bodies and Billions in Tax Dollars." *Philly.com*, 17 Aug. 2017, philly.com. Accessed 11 Dec. 2018.

7. "Prisons for Profit: Incarceration for Sale."

8. Alex Friedmann. "Apples-to-Fish: Public and Private Prison Cost Comparisons." *Prison Legal News*, 3 Oct. 2016, prisonlegalnews.org. Accessed 11 Dec. 2018.

9. Chris Kirkham. "Private Prison Empire Rises despite Startling Record of Juvenile Abuse." *Huffington Post*, 22 Oct. 2013, huffingtonpost.com. Accessed 11 Dec. 2018.

10. Pat Beall. "Whistleblower Suit Sheds Light on Decision to Dump Youth Contractor." *Palm Beach Post*, 4 Sept. 2016, palmbeachpost.com. Accessed 11 Dec. 2018.

11. Lauren-Brooke Eisen. *Inside Private Prisons*. Columbia UP, 2017. 59.

12. Bauer, "My Four Months as a Private Prison Guard."

13. Eisen, *Inside Private Prisons*, 58.

14. "20 Privatization of Prisons Pros and Cons." *Vittana*, n.d., vittana.org. Accessed 11 Dec. 2018.

15. Friedmann, "Apples-to-Fish."

16. Eisen, *Inside Private Prisons*, 59.

17. Chris Kirkham. "Lake Erie Prison Plagued by Violence and Drugs after Corporate Takeover." *Huffington Post*, 22 Mar. 2013, huffingtonpost.com. Accessed 11 Dec. 2018.

18. "14 Advantages and Disadvantages of Private Prisons." *Vittana*, n.d. vittana.org. Accessed 11 Dec. 2018.

19. King and Chen, "Private Prisons."

CHAPTER 4. PUBLIC VS. PRIVATE

1. Jordan King and Anthony Chen. "Private Prisons: An Evaluation of Economic and Ethical Implications." *Penn Wharton Public Policy Initiative*, 25 Jan. 2018, publicpolicy.wharton.upenn.edu. Accessed 11 Dec. 2018.

2. "Private Prisons in the United States." *Sentencing Project*, 2 Aug. 2018, sentencingproject.org. Accessed 11 Dec. 2018.

3. King and Chen, "Private Prisons."

4. King and Chen, "Private Prisons."

5. Christie Thompson. "Everything You Ever Wanted to Know about Private Prisons." *Marshall Project*, 18 Dec. 2014, themarshallproject.org. Accessed 11 Dec. 2018.

6. David E. Pozen. "Managing a Correctional Marketplace: Prison Privatization in the United States and the United Kingdom." *Journal of Law and Politics*, vol. 19, 274.

7. "Cost of Prisons: Bureau of Prisons Needs Better Data to Assess Alternatives for Acquiring Low and Minimum Security Facilities." *Government Accountability Office*, Oct. 2007, gao.gov. Accessed 11 Dec. 2018.

8. Alex Friedmann. "Apples-to-Fish: Public and Private Prison Cost Comparisons." *Prison Legal News*, 3 Oct. 2016, prisonlegalnews.org. Accessed 11 Dec. 2018.

9. "Biennial Comparison of 'Private Versus Public Provision of Services.'" *Arizona Department of Corrections*, 21 Dec. 2011, corrections.az.gov. Accessed 11 Dec. 2018.

10. Friedmann, "Apples-to-Fish."

11. Friedmann, "Apples-to-Fish."

12. Nathaniel Meyersohn. "Justice Department Seeks Increase in Private Prison Beds." *CNN*, 19 May 2017, cnn.com. Accessed 11 Dec. 2018.

13. Eric Lichtblau. "Justice Department Keeps For-Profit Prisons, Scrapping an Obama Plan." *New York Times*, 23 Feb. 2017, nytimes.com. Accessed 11 Dec. 2018.

14. Charles Chieppo. "The Pay-for-Performance Approach to Reducing Recidivism." *Governing*, 10 Sept. 2015, governing.com. Accessed 11 Dec. 2018.

15. Rikha Sharma Rani. "New Zealand Tries a Different Kind of Private Prison." *Citylab*, 31 Aug. 2017, citylab.com. Accessed 11 Dec. 2018.

16. "Private Prison Promises Leave Texas Towns in Trouble." *National Public Radio*, 28 March 2011, npr.org. Accessed 12 Dec. 2018.

SOURCE NOTES CONTINUED

CHAPTER 5. INMATE CARE

1. Jerry Mitchell. "Private Prisons Face Suits, Federal Probes." *Clarion Ledger*, 15 Oct. 2014, clarionledger.com. Accessed 11 Dec. 2018.

2. Christie Thompson. "Everything You Ever Wanted to Know about Private Prisons." *Marshall Project*, 18 Dec. 2014, themarshallproject.org. Accessed 11 Dec. 2018.

3. Alex Friedmann. "Apples-to-Fish: Public and Private Prison Cost Comparisons." *Prison Legal News*, 3 Oct. 2016, prisonlegalnews.org. Accessed 11 Dec. 2018.

4. Aleks Kajstura. "Women's Mass Incarceration: The Whole Pie 2017." *Prison Policy Initiative*, 19 Oct. 2017, prisonpolicy.org. Accessed 11 Dec. 2018.

5. "20 Privatization of Prisons Pros and Cons." *Vittana*, n.d., vittana.org. Accessed 11 Dec. 2018.

6. Beth Schwartzapfel. "How Bad Is Prison Health Care? Depends on Who's Watching." *Marshall Project*, 26 Feb. 2018, themarshallproject.org. Accessed 11 Dec. 2018.

7. "The Corrections Corporation of America, by the Numbers." *Mother Jones*, July/Aug. 2016, motherjones.com. Accessed 11 Dec. 2018.

8. Jacob Reich. "The Economic Impact of Prison Rehabilitation Programs." *Penn Wharton Public Policy Initiative*, 17 Aug. 2017, publicpolicy.wharton.upenn.edu. Accessed 11 Dec. 2018.

9. Reich, "The Economic Impact of Prison Rehabilitation Programs."

10. Lois M. Davis, et al. "Evaluating the Effectiveness of Correctional Education." *Rand Corporation*, 2013, rand.org. Accessed 11 Dec. 2018.

11. Reich, "The Economic Impact of Prison Rehabilitation Programs."

12. Judith Greene. "Comparing Private and Public Prison Services and Programs in Minnesota: Findings from Prisoner Interviews." *Current Issues in Criminal Justice*, n.d., inthepublicinterest.org. Accessed 11 Dec. 2018.

13. Reich, "The Economic Impact of Prison Rehabilitation Programs."

14. "5 out of 6 State Prisoners Were Arrested within 9 Years of Their Release." *Bureau of Justice Statistics*, 23 May 2018, bjs.gov. Accessed 11 Dec. 2018.

15. Friedmann, "Apples-to-Fish."

CHAPTER 6. PRISONS AND POLITICS

1. Azadeh Shahshahani. "Why Are For-Profit US Prisons Subjecting Detainees to Forced Labor?" *Guardian*, 17 May 2018, theguardian.com. Accessed 11 Dec. 2018.

2. Lauren-Brooke Eisen. *Inside Private Prisons*. Columbia UP, 2017. 185.

3. "Number of Registered Active Lobbyists in the United States from 2000 to 2017." *Statista*, 2018, statista.com. Accessed 11 Dec. 2018.

4. Sam Roberts. "Census Bureau's Counting of Prisoners Benefits Some Rural Voting Districts." *New York Times*, 23 Oct. 2008, nytimes.com. Accessed 11 Dec. 2018.

5. Alex Mayyasi. "How Does Prison Gerrymandering Work?" *Priceonomics*, 20 Oct. 2015, priceonomics.com. Accessed 11 Dec. 2018.

6. Amy Sherman. "Understanding Felon Voting Rights Restoration." *Politifact*, 25 Apr. 2018, politifact.com. Accessed 11 Dec. 2018.

CHAPTER 7. IMMIGRANT DETENTION

1. Lauren-Brooke Eisen. *Inside Private Prisons*. Columbia UP, 2017. 69.

2. Eisen, *Inside Private Prisons*, 147.

3. Eisen, *Inside Private Prisons*, 154.

4. "Detention Bed Quota." *National Immigrant Justice Center*, n.d., immigrantjustice.org. Accessed 11 Dec. 2018.

5. "Private Prisons in the United States." *Sentencing Project*, 2 Aug. 2018, sentencingproject.org. Accessed 11 Dec. 2018.

6. Juleyka Lantigua-Williams. "Feds End Use of Private Prisons, but Questions Remain." *Atlantic*, 18 Aug. 2016, theatlantic.com. Accessed 11 Dec. 2018.

7. Tara Tidwell Cullen. "ICE Released Its Most Comprehensive Immigration Detention Data Yet. It's Alarming." *National Immigrant Justice Center*, 13 Mar. 2018, immigrantjustice.org.

8. Eisen, *Inside Private Prisons*, 154.

9. Aimee Picchi. "One Winner under Trump: The Private Prison Industry." *CBS News*, 21 Feb. 2018, cbsnews.com. Accessed 11 Dec. 2018.

10. Reynaldo Leanos Jr. "A Private Prison Company with a Troubled Past Looks to Reopen an Immigration Detention Facility in Texas." *PRI*, 13 June 2017, pri.org. Accessed 11 Dec. 2018.

11. Picchi, "One Winner under Trump."

12. Alan Gomez. "Trump Plans Massive Increase in Federal Immigration Jails." *USA Today*, 17 Oct. 2017, usatoday.com. Accessed 11 Dec. 2018.

13. "ACLU Finds Abuse, Inhumane Conditions, at Little-Known Prisons for Immigrants Run by Private Companies for Federal Government." *ACLU*, 10 June 2014, aclu.org. Accessed 11 Dec. 2018.

14. Aaron Hegarty. "Timeline: Immigrant Children Separated from Families at the Border." *USA Today*, 25 July 2018, usatoday.com. Accessed 11 Dec. 2018.

15. Hegarty, "Timeline: Immigrant Children Separated from Families at the Border."

16. John Sepulvado. "More Than 360 Immigrant Children Still Separated from Their Parents." *National Public Radio*, 10 Aug. 2018, npr.org. Accessed 11 Dec. 2018.

CHAPTER 8. THE FUTURE OF FOR-PROFIT PRISONS

1. Eric Schlosser. "The Prison-Industrial Complex." *Atlantic*, Dec. 1998, theatlantic.com. Accessed 11 Dec. 2018.

2. Lauren-Brooke Eisen. *Inside Private Prisons*. Columbia UP, 2017. 185.

3. "Private Prisons in the United States." *Sentencing Project*, 2 Aug. 2018, sentencingproject.org. Accessed 11 Dec. 2018.

4. Eisen, *Inside Private Prisons*, 110.

5. Peter Edelman. *Not a Crime to Be Poor*. New Press, 2017. 49.

6. Gillian B. White. "Who Really Makes Money Off of Bail Bonds?" *Atlantic*, 12 May 2017, theatlantic.com. Accessed 11 Dec. 2018.

7. Edelman, *Not a Crime to Be Poor*, 31.

8. Edelman, *Not a Crime to Be Poor*, 8.

9. "Incorrect Care: A Prison Profiteer Turns Care into Confinement." *Grassroots Leadership*, Feb. 2016, grassrootsleadership.org. Accessed 11 Dec. 2018.

10. "Incorrect Care."

11. "20 Privatization of Prisons Pros and Cons." *Vittana*, n.d., vittana.org. Accessed 11 Dec. 2018.

12. Jordan King and Anthony Chen. "Private Prisons: An Evaluation of Economic and Ethical Implications." *Penn Wharton Public Policy Initiative*, 25 Jan. 2018, publicpolicy.wharton.upenn.edu. Accessed 11 Dec. 2018.

13. "Private Prisons in the United States."

INDEX

ABOUT THE AUTHORS

DUCHESS HARRIS, JD, PHD

Dr. Harris is a professor of American Studies at Macalester College and curator of the Duchess Harris Collection of ABDO books. She is also the coauthor of the titles in the collection, which features popular selections such as *Hidden Human Computers: The Black Women of NASA* and series including News Literacy and Being Female in America.

Before working with ABDO, Dr. Harris authored several other books on the topics of race, culture, and American history. She served as an associate editor for *Litigation News*, the American Bar Association Section of Litigation's quarterly flagship publication, and was the first editor in chief of *Law Raza*, an interactive online journal covering race and the law, published at William Mitchell College of Law. She has earned a PhD in American Studies from the University of Minnesota and a JD from William Mitchell College of Law.

CYNTHIA KENNEDY HENZEL

Cynthia Kennedy Henzel has a BS in social studies education and an MS in geography. She has worked as a teacher-educator in many countries. Currently, she writes books and develops education materials for social studies, history, science, and ELL students. She has written more than 85 books for young people.